Searchlight
BOOKS™

How
Does Energy
Work?

Investigating
Sound

Sally M. Walker

Lerner Publications Company
Minneapolis

Author's note: The experiments in this book use the metric measurement system, as that's the system most commonly used by scientists.

Lerner Publications Company
A division of Lerner Publishing Group, Inc.
241 First Avenue North
Minneapolis, MN 55401 U.S.A.

Website address: www.lernerbooks.com

Library of Congress Cataloging-in-Publication Data

Investigating sound / by Sally M. Walker.
    p.   cm. — (Searchlight books™—How does energy work?)
Includes index.
ISBN 978–0–7613–5777–3 (lib. bdg. : alk. paper)
1. Sound—Juvenile literature. 2. Sound waves—Juvenile literature. I. Title.
QC225.5.W3154 2012
534—dc22   2010040529

Manufactured in the United States of America
1 – DP – 7/15/11

Contents

Chapter 1

WHAT IS SOUND?

Clap your hands. Whisper your name. What do you hear? You hear a sound. Some sounds are nice to hear. But a sound like a fingernail scraping a chalkboard bothers many people. We call sounds that bother us noise.

We like some sounds better than other sounds. What do we call sounds that bother us?

This excavator is part of a noisy construction site.

Animals make sounds. So do machines. The wind blowing through trees makes a sound. What causes sound?

Sound begins when an object moves back and forth very quickly. The movements are called vibrations.

Try This!

Loop a rubber band around your thumbs. Pluck the rubber band with your pinkie finger. This makes a sound.

Watch the band. You can see it vibrate. The vibrations move through the air to your ears. Then you hear the sound.

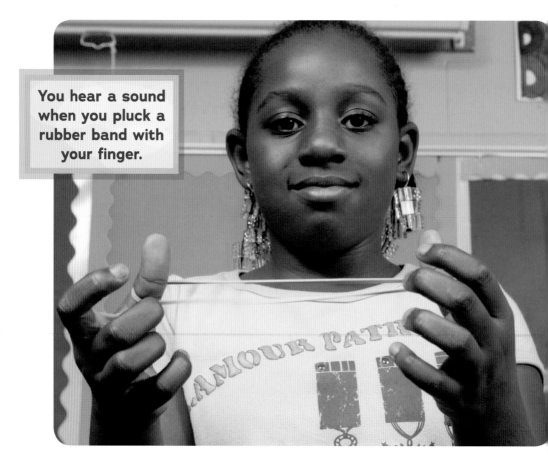

You hear a sound when you pluck a rubber band with your finger.

You can feel vibrations too. Put one hand on top of your head and hum loudly. The tingling feeling in your hand is from the vibrations you make when you hum.

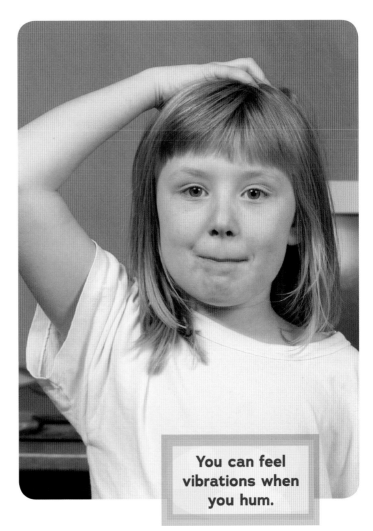

You can feel vibrations when you hum.

Sound Moves through Matter

Sound goes from place to place by moving through matter. Anything that can be weighed or takes up space is called matter. Matter makes up everything around you. Matter can be a solid, like a table or a chair. Matter can be a liquid, like water. Or it can be a gas. The air you breathe is a gas.

Matter is all around you. This book is a solid.

Matter is made of tiny particles called atoms. A single atom is too small to see with your eyes. Billions of them can fit on the period at the end of this sentence. Atoms join together to make molecules. For example, one molecule of water has two atoms of hydrogen and one atom of oxygen.

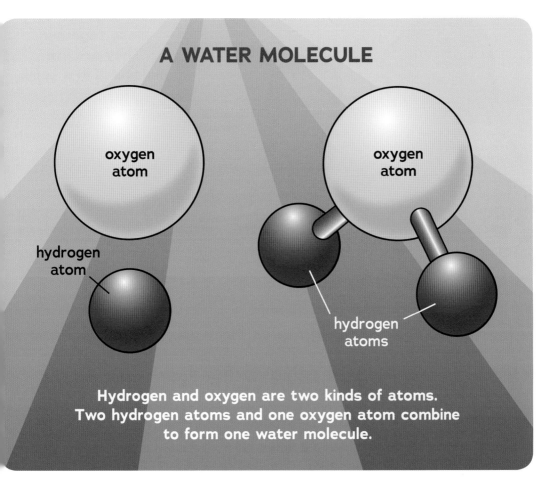

A WATER MOLECULE

oxygen atom

hydrogen atom

oxygen atom

hydrogen atoms

Hydrogen and oxygen are two kinds of atoms. Two hydrogen atoms and one oxygen atom combine to form one water molecule.

Molecules in Solids, Liquids, and Gases

Molecules are always moving. But molecules move in different ways in solids, liquids, and gases.

Molecules that are packed tightly together can't move very much. They form a solid. Tightly packed water molecules make ice. Ice is a solid.

These kids are very close together. They are like molecules in a solid.

These kids have lots of space to move around. They are like molecules in a gas.

Molecules that are less tightly packed make a liquid. Molecules in a liquid can move freely. That's why you can pour water from a glass into a bowl.

Molecules in a gas are spread out and move even more freely. They are so spread out that we can't see them. We can't see air. But we can see what happens when the air moves. Moving air is wind.

Chapter 2

SOUND WAVES

The molecules in all kinds of matter vibrate when something makes a sound. The vibrations are called sound waves. A toy called a Slinky can show you how sound waves move.

The pictures on these pages show how a wave moves along a Slinky. How are sound waves like the wave moving in the Slinky?

Experiment Time

Place the Slinky on a table. Stretch the ends about 0.6 meters apart. Quickly slide one hand about 7 centimeters toward the other hand.

A wave will move along the Slinky. The wave pushes through each coil and makes it vibrate. The coil stops moving after the wave passes. Sound waves move from one molecule to the next just as the wave moves from one coil to the next.

The movement of your hand makes the Slinky vibrate. You see the vibration as a wave that moves from one end to the other.

A Slinky's wave moves in only one direction. But sound waves spread in all directions. They get weaker when they spread. Prove it yourself.

Now Try This!

Ask a friend to stand about 8 meters away from you. Whisper to your friend. Your whisper's sound waves spread in all directions. Only some of the sound waves move toward your friend. Spreading makes them weak. That's why your friend can't hear you.

Sound waves spread out like the waves you see in a pool of water.

You can stop the sound waves from spreading out. You will need a garden hose. Make sure no water is inside the hose. Have your friend hold one end near his ear. You hold the other end. Whisper into the hose. Can your friend hear you?

Do not shout through the hose, or you could hurt your friend's ear.

The hose keeps your sound waves from spreading and becoming weaker. Almost all of them reach your friend's ear.

You can also make sound waves bounce. A ball thrown against a wall will bounce off. A sound wave will bounce off a hard surface too. Stand in the middle of an empty room. Shout. You will hear an echo of your shout. An echo is a reflected sound wave.

The sound waves from your shout moved from your mouth to the room's walls. Then the sound waves bounced off the walls and traveled back to you.

A ball bounces off a solid wall. So do sound waves. You can make sound echo in an empty room.

Some objects carry sound better than others. Find a metal pan, a kitchen towel, and a metal spoon.

Hold the handle of the metal pan. Tap the bottom of the pan with the spoon. It rings like a bell. The pan's metal molecules are tightly packed. Sound waves move strongly from one molecule to the next.

The metal pan and the metal spoon are both solids.

Fold the towel and set it on a table. Tap it with the spoon. This time, you hear a thud. The molecules that make the towel are not as tightly packed as metal molecules. The molecules in the towel have air around them. The sound waves spread and weaken when they move through the towel.

The towel is a solid. But it also has spaces where air can get in it.

Chapter 3

THE SPEED OF SOUND

You see lightning before you hear thunder because light waves travel faster than sound waves. How fast do sound waves travel?

How fast do sound waves move? A sound made 1 mile (1.6 kilometers) away from you takes about five seconds to reach you. It moves at about 1,056 feet (322 m) per second. That's pretty fast!

Sound waves move faster on a hot day than they do on a cold day. Air molecules bump into one another more often when the air is hot. So sound waves can move from one molecule to the next more quickly.

Hot air molecules move quickly. They run into one another a lot, just like these kids.

Sound Waves and Solids, Liquids, and Gases

Sound waves move at different speeds through liquids, solids, and gases. Sound waves travel four times faster in water than they do in air. That's because water molecules are closer together than air molecules. A sound wave can move from one water molecule to the next very quickly.

Sound waves move through water very quickly.

Molecules of wood are even closer together than water molecules. So it takes even less time for a sound wave to move from one wood molecule to the next. Sound waves travel about thirteen times faster in wood than they do in air.

Sound waves move through wood even faster than they move through water.

You can prove that sound moves faster in a solid than in a gas.

Experiment Time Again!

Test the speed of sound in a solid wall. Ask a friend to stand at one end of a room. Stand at the other end. Ask your friend to tap the wall with a pen.

The sound you hear is not very loud. The air molecules between you and your friend carry the sound wave slowly. The sound has time to spread out and get weaker. Put your ear against the wall. Listen again. The taps are much louder. Why? The sound waves move quickly through the wall's tightly packed molecules. The sound does not have time to spread out and get weak.

Chapter 4

MAKING MUSIC

How fast an object vibrates changes the sound it makes. Usually, objects that vibrate fast make high sounds. We describe the high sound by saying it has a high pitch.

You can make a high sound with a rubber band. What makes the sound high or low?

Testing It Out

Stretch a rubber band tightly between your thumbs. Pluck it with your pinkie. The twang has a high pitch. The band vibrates very fast.

Move your thumbs together until the rubber band is hardly stretched. Pluck it again. The sound is much lower. That's because the band is vibrating more slowly. We describe the lower sound by saying it has a low pitch.

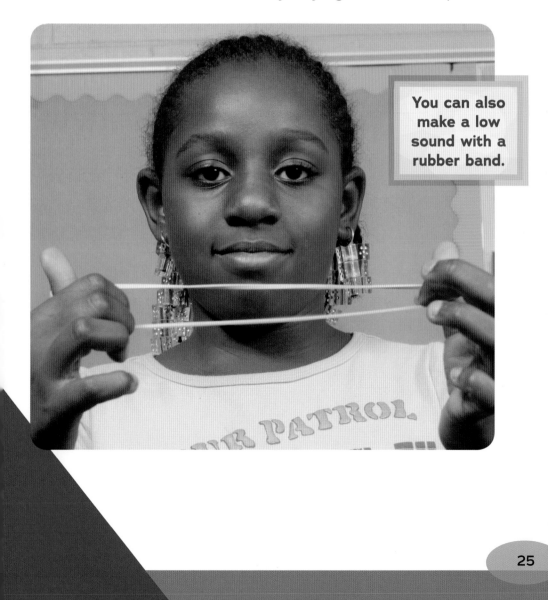

You can also make a low sound with a rubber band.

Music has sounds with many different pitches. You can blow across a drinking straw to make a sound. A short straw has a different pitch than a long one. Short straws have higher pitches. Long ones have lower pitches.

Blowing across a straw makes a sound. So does blowing across the opening of a bottle.

Straw Flute

Make a straw flute, and prove this for yourself. You will need eight plastic drinking straws, a ruler, a marker, a scissors, tape, and a 15-centimeter square of cardboard.

Measure one straw with the ruler. It is probably 19.5 centimeters long. You can cut the straw if it is longer. Use your marker to make a line on the straw at 19.5 centimeters. Cut the straw on the line. Write the number 1 on the straw.

Measure carefully so that your straw flute will sound good when you finish it.

Measure, cut, and number the other seven straws. Their numbers and lengths should be as follows:

#2 = 18 centimeters

#3 = 16 centimeters

#4 = 14.5 centimeters

#5 = 12.5 centimeters

#6 = 11.5 centimeters

#7 = 10 centimeters

#8 = 9.5 centimeters

You will need to use a sharp pair of scissors. Ask an adult for help if you have trouble cutting the straws.

Tape the straws to the cardboard. Tape straw #1 along one edge of the cardboard. Make sure the straw sticks up a little bit over the top end of the cardboard. Tape straw #8 at the other edge of the cardboard. It should also stick up a little bit.

Try to make sure all the straws stick up about 1 centimeter over one side of the cardboard.

Put the rest of the straws on the cardboard between straws #1 and #8. The straws should be in order from longest to shortest. Tape the straws so that they stick up over the cardboard the same amount as straws #1 and #8.

Each straw will make a sound with a different pitch.

When you blow across a straw, you make the air inside the straw vibrate. This makes a sound.

Your flute is finished. Hold the cardboard with the ends of the straws near your bottom lip. Blow across the hole at the top of each straw. The pitch of each straw is different. Why? The air in each straw vibrates at a different speed when you blow. Try to play a song on your new flute.

Chapter 5

SOUNDS WE CAN'T HEAR

People hear sound when an object vibrates. But we can't hear some sounds. We don't hear anything if an object vibrates less than twenty times per second.

You can wave your hand back and forth rapidly—but not faster than twenty times per second. So you don't hear a sound. The lowest notes on a piano are close to twenty vibrations per second.

This girl can't hear her hands flapping. What are sounds we can't hear called?

Infrasounds

Sounds made by vibrations of less than twenty times per second are called infrasounds. Thunderstorms and earthquakes can make infrasounds. We know about them because special instruments record and measure them.

Elephants make infrasounds to communicate with other elephants that are very far away.

Each key on the piano plays a note with a different vibration.

We can hear sounds made by objects that vibrate back and forth as many as twenty thousand times per second. The very highest note on a piano vibrates about fifteen thousand times per second.

Ultrasounds

Sounds made by vibrations of more than twenty thousand times per second are called ultrasounds. Bats make ultrasound waves.

Bats fly at night, when it is too dark to see. So they use ultrasound waves to help them. The ultrasounds hit objects such as the ground, tree branches, and insects. Then the sounds echo back to the bat. The echoes tell the bat where to fly. An ultrasound wave bounces off an insect. Then the bat can catch the insect and eat it!

Bats use sound to help them fly at night.

Listen!

You have learned a lot about sound. Matter vibrates when a sound is made. Sound travels in waves. Sounds can have high or low pitches.

You can make the strings on a guitar vibrate. This makes music.

Sit or stand still quietly for a minute. Close your eyes. Listen carefully. What can you hear? Hopefully, something that sounds good!

You hear many sounds all day long. What is your favorite sound?

Glossary

atom: a very tiny particle that makes up all things

echo: a sound that is heard again after sound waves hit a surface and bounce back

infrasound: a sound that is too low-pitched for people to hear

matter: anything that takes up space and can be weighed. All things are made of matter.

molecule: the smallest amount of a substance that can be found

noise: a loud or harsh sound

pitch: how high or low a musical note sounds

reflected: bounced back from a surface

sound wave: a vibration that can be heard or measured

ultrasound: a sound that is too high-pitched for people to hear

vibration: a quick movement back and forth

Learn More about Sound

Books

Brasch, Nicolas. *Why Does Sound Travel?: All about Sound.* New York: PowerKids Press, 2010. This book offers an interesting discussion of sound.

Lawrence, Mary. *What's That Sound?* New York: Kane Press, 2002. In this fun mystery from the Science Solves It! series, Tim is spooked when he hears scary noises in the house.

Waring, Geoff. *Oscar and the Bat: A Book about Sound.* Cambridge, MA: Candlewick Press, 2008. Waring takes a playful look at sound in this title.

Woodford, Chris. *Experiments with Sound and Hearing.* New York: Gareth Stevens, 2010. Check out this book to find more experiments related to sound.

Websites

Enchanted Learning: Ear Anatomy Diagram
http://www.enchantedlearning.com/subjects/anatomy/ear
Find a labeled diagram of the human ear, along with information on how our ears help us hear.

Neuroscience for Kids: Hearing Experiments
http://faculty.washington.edu/chudler/chhearing.html
This page includes information about the ear and hearing, along with fun sound experiments to try.

The Science of Music
http://www.exploratorium.edu/music/index.html
Learn more about music while using this fun site to make music of your own.

Index

Photo Acknowledgments

Photographs copyright © Andy King. Additional images in this book are used with the permission of: © Tetsuya Yamada/Bloomberg/Getty Images, p. 5; © Laura Westlund/Independent Picture Service, p. 9; © Steve Allen/The Image Bank/Getty Images, p. 33; © Stephen Dalton/Minden Pictures, p. 35; © Canettistock/Dreamstime.com, p. 36.

Front Cover: © momentimages/Getty Images.

Main body text set in Adrianna Regular 14/20.
Typeface provided by Chank.